# THE HOW AND WHY WONDER BOOK OF
# MAGNETS
# AND MAGNETISM

Written by
MARTIN L. KEEN

Illustrated by
GEORGE ZAFFO

Editorial Production:
DONALD D. WOLF

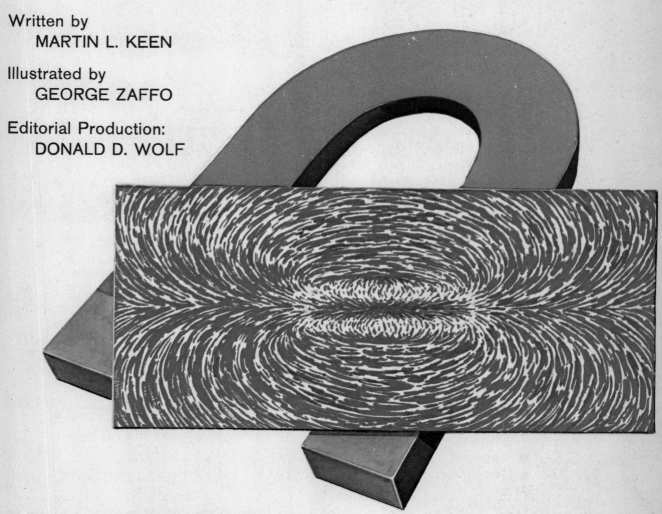

Edited under the supervision of
Dr. Paul E. Blackwood, Washington, D.C.

Text and illustrations approved by
Oakes A. White, Brooklyn Children's Museum, Brooklyn, New York

**WONDER BOOKS · NEW YORK**

# Introduction

Through the ages, magnetism has held a fascination for everyone. The allure of magnets continues to this day. Any boy or girl with a magnet will be engrossed with it for many an hour. And, if father and mother have a chance, they will experiment with it too. This *How and Why Wonder Book of Magnets and Magnetism* will help boys, girls, fathers, and mothers satisfy their curiosity about the mysterious force of magnetism.

It is very easy to find out what magnets will do, yet it is far from obvious what magnetism is. With the knowledge of what magnets do, scientists and inventors have developed hundreds of practical ways of using them in our homes and in industry.

In magnetism, we have an excellent example of a physical phenomenon that is useful even though much remains to be learned about it. Gravity is another such example. Both are puzzling but very useful forces. In each case, the challenge to scientists is to probe deeper and to learn more about them.

This *How and Why Wonder Book of Magnets and Magnetism* systematically summarizes much that is known about magnets. At the same time, it suggests that a great deal remains to be learned. Perhaps it will stimulate young readers to become partners of scientists in the never-ending search for knowledge. And that is the method of scientists — always investigating unknown questions, always seeking answers.

*Paul E. Blackwood*

Dr. Blackwood is a professional employee in the U. S. Office of Education. This book was edited by him in his private capacity and no official support or endorsement by the Office of Education is intended or should be inferred.

# Contents

## MAGNETISM:

In a junk yard, a crane lowers a thick metal disc into a pile of scrap metal. When the disc is raised, the body of an automobile and a few large pieces of iron are attached to it, although no chains or ropes hold these things in place. A refrigerator door is held tightly closed, although it has no latch or lock. Button-sized pieces of metal hold a sheet of paper on a bulletin board with nothing apparently holding them up. In all these instances magnetism is at work.

Your phone rings and then your friend's voice tells you that he is coming to your house. Soon your doorbell rings,

The crane in the junk-yard lifting an automobile, the telephone, the doorbell, the television screen you watch, and the beautiful display of colored lights you may have seen in the northern or southern skies, all have to do, one way or another, with magnetism.

as your friend arrives. Then the two of you watch the images of football players rush back and forth across your television screen. The phone, the doorbell, and the television set could not work if it were not for magnets and magnetism.

You may have seen, in the direction of the polar regions, great glowing curtains of varicolored light sweeping across the night sky. You know these curtains are the northern lights, or *aurora borealis,* or their southern counterpart, the *aurora australis.* This vast display of lights is due to magnetism.

Magnetism plays an increasingly important part in our daily lives as we use more and more household appliances and electrical devices. Scientists probing further and further into the secrets of nature find magnetism to be important everywhere, whether it be within the extremely small nucleus of an atom or in the vast distances of the astronomical universe. Let us investigate this phenomenon we call magnetism by reading about it on the following pages and by performing experiments that help us to understand what we read.

A legend tells us that the word "magnetism" comes from Magnes, a Greek shepherd, whose staff clung to a "magnetic stone."

# The Nature of Magnetism

A *magnet* is a piece of metal that has certain unique properties. A magnet can pull toward itself, and hold, pieces of iron. For instance, a small hand-held magnet can pull and hold nails, screws, paper clips, and other things made of iron or steel, which is a kind of iron. A magnet can pull another magnet toward itself or push the other magnet away. What is so remarkable about a magnet is that it can perform its work without actually touching the objects that it pulls or pushes.

**What are magnets and magnetism?**

We say objects that act like magnets are *magnetized*. The invisible something that enables magnets to pull or push other objects is called *magnetism*. Magnetism cannot be seen, heard, smelled, tasted, or directly felt, and it does not have any weight. Because magnetism cannot be detected by our senses, the only way we can learn anything about it is by noting what it does.

The two kinds of magnets that we will work with are *bar magnets,* which are short straight pieces of metal, and *horseshoe magnets* which are bar mag-

BAR MAGNET

HORSESHOE MAGNET

nets bent into the shape of a horseshoe or the letter U. You can buy magnets in toy stores, hobby shops, and hardware stores.

There is a legend that in ancient Greece

**How did magnetism get its name?** a shepherd boy named Magnes, while tending his sheep on Mount Ida, placed his staff on a large stone and found that the stone clung to the tip of the staff so strongly that Magnes could not pull the stone free. The legend goes on to say that from Magnes' name we get the name "magnet," because of a magnetic stone that clung to Magnes' staff. The following explanation is probably closer to the truth. The word "magnet" comes from the name of the city of Magnesia in Asia Minor, near which magnetic stones, or, more accurately, pieces of magnetic iron ore, were found in abundance. The modern name for magnetic iron ore is *magnetite*.

The Greeks and Romans knew that a piece of magnetite would attract small pieces of iron even through a bronze or wooden bowl, or when under water. Many strange beliefs grew up about a substance as curious as magnetite. The ancients believed that charms and finger rings made of magnetic stones could attract one's beloved, and that a piece of magnetite placed on your head would make you able to hear the voices of the gods. Magnetic stones also were believed to cure rheumatism, cramps, or gout. Powdered magnetite mixed with oil or grease was said to prevent or cure baldness.

During the Middle Ages, pieces of magnetic iron ore were called *load-stones,* or *lodestones*. They continued to be regarded as amulets and interesting curiosities until someone observed that when a loadstone is suspended by a thread, one end of the loadstone always points north.

Mariners soon made use of this fact. They understood that if one end of a suspended loadstone always points north, then a ship with such a loadstone aboard can always be guided in the direction desired, even when the sun, moon, and stars are hidden by clouds. Loadstone got its name from being used for direction-finding. "Load" was an old English word for "way," and a load-stone was a "way-finding stone."

The ancients attributed to magnets many supernatural qualities that could be used for curing a large number of ills.

One day, somebody discovered that one end of a loadstone, suspended by a thread, always points north.

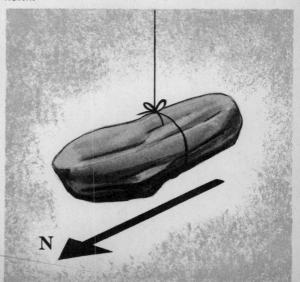

N

Mariners of the past were afraid of the "mountain of loadstone" which, as the legend goes, could wreck even the most seaworthy vessels.

At left, a primitive compass, consisting of a magnetized needle on a cork floating in water. Columbus used such a compass.

a large needle (by stroking it on a loadstone) and then thrusting the needle through a piece of reed or cork so that it would float when placed in a bowl filled with water. One end of the needle always pointed north, and this was the first real compass needle.

Even before loadstone was used to guide ships, mariners had a legend about it. They believed that there was a great Mountain of Loadstone. No one knew

The suspended loadstone was the first compass. Actually, a piece of loadstone hung by a thread did not make a completely satisfactory compass. It was not long before mariners devised a more sensitive compass by magnetizing

just where this mountain was located, but it was feared by all mariners who sailed the seas of the Far East. The mariners believed that if a ship sailed too close, the Mountain of Loadstone would attract every piece of iron on board the ship. This would draw the ship irresistibly toward the mountain. As the ship drew closer, all loose pieces of iron would fly straight out to the mountain. Finally, when the ship was very close, the mountain would pull the bolts and nails out of the ship's timbers, and the ship would fall apart. Sinbad the Sailor, one of the heroes in *The Arabian Nights,* was shipwrecked by the Mountain of Loadstone.

**What are magnetic poles?** If you suspend a bar magnet horizontally by a loop of thread, as shown in the illustration, you will find that when the magnet stops swinging, one end will point north. This end is the *north-seeking pole,* or simply *north pole,* of the magnet. The other end of the magnet is the *south-seeking,* or *south pole.* The north pole may be

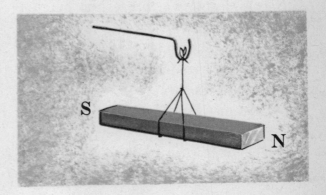

called simply the "N pole," and the south pole the "S pole." No matter in what direction the ends of the magnet may point when you suspend it, and no matter how many times you may perform this experiment, one end will always point north. Later, we will learn why this is so.

Perhaps the first account of the use of the magnet for finding direction comes from China at the time of Hoang-ti, who reigned over his empire nearly 5000 years ago. Pursuing a rebellious prince, he became lost in a dense fog. He found both his way and the enemy by guiding a wonderful chariot he had constructed. Mounted on the front of this chariot was the figure of a woman that could swivel in all directions and that always pointed with one outstretched arm to the south, regardless of the direction in which the chariot was driven. If the legend is true, there must have been a magnet in the figure. (While the western world considers the needle of the compass to point north, the Chinese consider the compass needle as pointing south.)

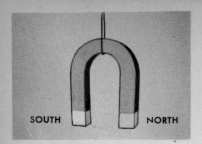

One side of a suspended horseshoe magnet will always point to the north.

If you suspend a horseshoe magnet by a loop of thread around the middle of the horseshoe curve, you will find that when the magnet stops swinging, one side of the horseshoe will always point north. Since we learned that a horseshoe magnet is a bar magnet bent into the shape of a horseshoe, you can easily understand that the north pole of the horseshoe magnet is at the end of the side that points north.

Now is a good time to mark the north and south poles of your magnets. Suspend each magnet by a thread. As soon as you know which is the north pole, mark it on the magnet with an N; mark the other pole with an S. Use pencil, ink, or crayon — whichever will write on your magnet.

**What is the Law of Magnetic Poles?**

Suspend a magnet as you did when marking its poles. Note which end of the suspended magnet is its N pole. Take another magnet in hand, and, beginning at a distance of ten inches, slowly approach the N pole of the suspended magnet with the S pole of the magnet in your hand. Soon, you will see the end of the suspended magnet move toward the end of the approaching magnet. If you turn the magnet in your hand around so that its N pole approaches the N pole of the suspended magnet, you will see the suspended magnet swing away from the approaching magnet.

Repeat what you have just done, first, approaching the S pole of the suspended magnet with the N pole of the magnet in your hand. Then approach the S pole of the suspended magnet with the S pole of the magnet in your hand. Note whether the suspended magnet swings toward or away from the approaching magnet each time.

On a sheet of paper print the following table and record by means of check marks in the proper column just how the magnets acted in the experiment you just performed. If necessary, repeat the experiment. Your check marks should appear in the same places as those in the table printed on the bottom of page 11.

What do the locations of the check marks show? They show that *unlike magnetic poles* (a north pole and a south pole) *attract one another, and like magnetic poles* (two north poles or two south poles) *repel one another.* This is the Law of Magnetic Poles.

Experiments to demonstrate the Law of Magnetic Poles.

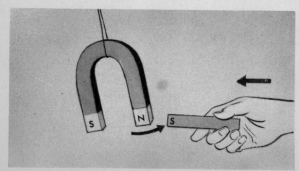

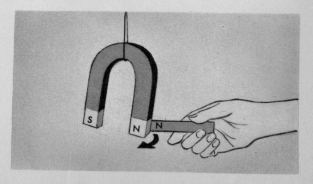

To perform this experiment you will

**How can you cause magnets to float in air?**

need two powerful magnets of the kind known as alnico magnets. (Alnico magnets are made of a special kind of metal. You will read more about alnico magnets in another part of this book.)

If you are going to use bar magnets, you will have to make a guide frame in the following manner. Obtain six small sticks about five inches long, such as ice-cream or lollipop sticks. You can also use six pencils. Place a bar magnet on the center of the top of a small cardboard box. Make two pencil marks evenly spaced on either side of the magnet, and two marks a sixteenth of an inch out from each end of the magnet. Now push a stick through both the top and bottom of the box at each pencil mark. Finally, place the second magnet into the frame of sticks surrounding the first magnet. Be sure the north pole of the upper magnet is above the north pole of the lower magnet; then, of course, south pole will be above south pole. The upper magnet will remain suspended in the air, as if by magic. But you know that the reason why the upper magnet hangs unsupported. Like magnetic poles are repelling each other, as we learned they do when we learned the Law of Magnetic Poles.

If you use horseshoe magnets, you will have to make your guide frame as shown in the second illustration on this page.

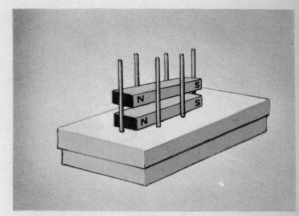

Magnets that "float on air."

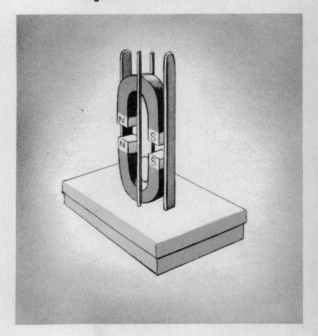

| Pole of suspended magnet | Pole of approaching magnet | Poles swing toward (*attract*) one another | Poles swing away from (*repel*) one another |
|---|---|---|---|
| N | S | ✓ | |
| N | N | | ✓ |
| S | N | ✓ | |
| S | S | | ✓ |

Go around your house trying to pick up different small

**What are magnetic materials?**

objects with your magnets. Try to pick up paper clips, pencils, erasers, rubber bands. See whether your magnets will pick up pieces of paper, wood, plastic, cloth. Try to pick up pebbles, grains of sand, salt, and sugar. See whether you can pick up a nickel, a dime, a quarter.

All the objects that your magnets pick up are made of *magnetic materials*. A magnetic material is one that can be attracted by a magnet. The main magnetic materials are the metals, iron, nickel, and cobalt. Of these three, iron is by far the most magnetic. But there are also mixtures of metals, called alloys, that make materials far more magnetic than iron. Alnico is the name of an alloy made of aluminum, nickel, iron, cobalt, and copper. We learned that we needed very strong or alnico magnets in order to make a magnet float in air.

The more magnetic a material is, the stronger the magnet that can be made of it. Also, the more strongly magnetic a material is, the more easily it is attracted by a magnet. Probably the most magnetic material of all is an alloy that is four-fifths platinum and one-fifth cobalt.

Although there are other magnetic materials, the objects your magnets picked up around your house were probably made of iron or steel. As we have learned, steel is a kind of iron. Materials that are not magnetic are said to be *non-magnetic*.

You probably know that dishonest per-

**How does a vending machine reject slugs?**

sons may try to buy candy, peanuts, ice cream, soda, or other things from vending machines by putting slugs into the coin slot. A slug is a metal washer or other flat circular piece of metal the size of a coin and usually made of iron or steel. To prevent this kind of stealing, the manufacturers build devices into their vending machines that cause the machine to reject slugs. If a slug is put into one of these vending machines, it simply falls through the machine to the coin-return slot, and no merchandise can be obtained from the machine.

Slug rejectors work in different ways. Some vending machines have more than one kind of slug rejector. The following is a description of three kinds of slug-rejectors — two non-magnetic and one magnetic — that may be built into a vending machine. When a coin or slug is put into the coin slot, it rolls down a narrow channel. This channel has a hole just a little smaller than the size of the required coin. A coin rolls over this hole, but a slug smaller than the coin falls through the hole and goes to the coin-return slot. Farther down the channel is a spring attached to a piece of metal blocking the way. The spring cannot be moved by a slug that is lighter than the required coin. A light slug bounces off the piece of metal and falls to the coin-return slot. A slug that goes past the first two slug-rejectors comes to a magnetic slug rejector. Here, the coin or slug, continuing to fall down the narrow channel comes to a branch in the shape of an upside-down V, like this ∧. There is a magnet at the top of one of the branches. When a steel slug falls to the top of the branch in the channel, the slug is pulled down the branch that contains the magnet. The magnet is just strong enough to pull the slug, but not to hold it, so the slug continues down the branch into which it was pulled and then on to the coin-return slot. Coins roll down the other branch of the inverted V, where they release the merchandise.

When you were going around your house testing objects to learn which were made of magnetic materials, you found that coins were non-magnetic. You can see that in a magnetic slug-rejector a coin will not be pulled into the channel that has the magnet.

**How can you make a magnetic slug rejector?** To make a magnetic slug rejector, you will need a strong magnet, a piece of stiff cardboard about the size of a page of this book, some nickels, dimes, or pennies, and a supply of three-quarter-inch steel washers. You can buy the washers at a hardware store.

Draw a line down the middle of both sides of the piece of cardboard. Use adhesive cellophane tape to attach a magnet half an inch from the middle line and halfway from top to bottom of the piece of cardboard. Use some books to prop the cardboard at an angle, as shown in the illustration, with the magnet on the underside.

One by one, place the coins and the slugs at the center of the top of the cardboard, and let them slide down. Just what happens now will depend on how strong your magnet is. If it is weak, it will push the steel washers sidewise a

## HOW TO MAKE A SLUG REJECTOR.

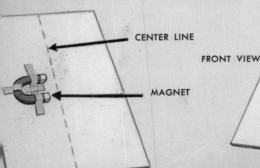

CENTER LINE

FRONT VIEW

MAGNET

BACK VIEW

FRONT VIEW

COINS

WASHERS

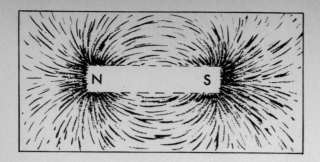

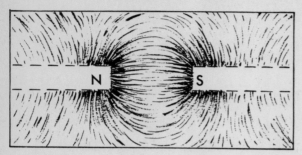

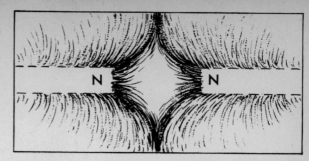

Patterns of lines of magnetic force created by (top left) one bar magnet, (left) two bar magnets with unlike poles opposite each other, (above) two bar magnets with like poles opposite each other.

little bit as they slide past. If the magnet is of medium strength, it will push the washers farther out of the straight-line path down the cardboard. If your magnet is strong, it will hold the steel washers as they reach it in their slide down the cardboard. No matter what the strength of the magnet, the coins will slide past it. Thus, your magnetic slug rejector has separated the slugs from the coins by either pushing the coins sideways, as though into a coin-return channel, or by keeping the slugs from following the coins.

You may wonder why a magnetic slug rejector does not reject nickels, because these coins must certainly be made of nickel, a metal which we learned is magnetic. The answer is that the metal of which a nickel is made is a mixture that is three-fourths copper and one-fourth nickel, and the resulting alloy is only very slightly magnetic.

You have learned that you become

**What are lines of magnetic force?** aware of magnetism by noting what it does. Now, give magnetism something to do;

make it write its signature. You need a magnet, a sheet of stiff paper (thin cardboard or a thin plate of glass can be used), and about a teaspoonful of iron filings or any other form of iron dust.

If you know someone who works in a machine shop, he will probably give you all the filings you need. Perhaps you know someone who has a grinding wheel and can provide iron particles with little trouble by grinding them from a piece of iron. If you must make your own iron filings, you will find it easy, although a little tiresome. Obtain a large iron nail or any other piece of iron. A carpenter will probably be glad to give you one or two large nails. If possible, clamp the nail firmly in a machinist's vise. If you do not have the use of a vise, hold one end of the nail firmly on a hard surface (not a polished table top!). Place a large sheet of paper beneath the nail to catch the filings. To file the nail, use a medium-coarse machinist's file. Ask a hardware dealer about this kind of file. Be sure not to use a wood file. Now, simply file and file and file, until you have enough iron filings. If you have a hacksaw, you will find that cutting the nail into several pieces is another way to provide yourself with sufficient iron powder from the iron sawdust.

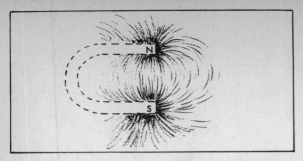
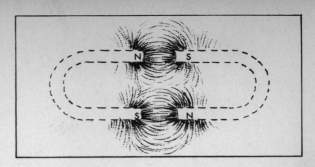
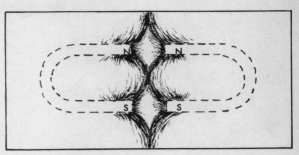

Lines of magnetic force created by, (above) one horseshoe magnet, (top right) two horseshoe magnets unlike poles opposite each other, (right) two horseshoe magnets with like poles opposite each other.

Put a magnet on a table and place your sheet of stiff paper so that it rests upon the magnet. Sprinkle the iron particles slowly and evenly upon the paper, covering the area just above, and for two or three inches on all sides of the magnet. Then, tap the paper lightly several times with a pencil point in order to make certain that the iron particles are spread evenly.

If you have used a bar magnet, the iron particles will arrange themselves in the pattern shown in illustration A on page 14. If you have used a horseshoe magnet, the arrangement of iron particles will be that shown in illustration A at the top of page 15. Lines of iron particles radiate outward from both poles of the magnet. Scientists say that the particles are arranged along *lines of magnetic force.* No one knows exactly what lines of magnetic force are, but they are always present near a magnet. They are invisible, but by making them reveal themselves in a pattern by means of iron particles, you cause the lines of magnetic force to write their signature.

Try the same experiment again, this time placing the north and south poles of two magnets half an inch to an inch apart. Now the lines of magnetic force arrange the iron particles as shown in illustration B on page 14, if you have

used bar magnets, and as shown in illustration B on page 15, if you have used horseshoe magnets.

Repeat the experiment once more, this time placing like poles near each other. The particles will be lined up as shown in illustration C on page 14, if you have used bar magnets, and as in illustration C on page 15, if you have used horseshoe magnets.

Note that in all three experiments, the iron particles are thickest at the poles of a magnet. Careful measurements have shown that each pole occupies about one-twelfth the length of a magnet.

Why do we say that the iron filings in the experiment you just performed are arranged by lines of magnetic force? Because when any object is moved or kept from falling, or when an elastic object is bent, stretched, or compressed, we say that a force is acting. You know that a magnet can move magnetic materials without touching them, and it can keep them from falling. You have seen a paper clip jump

**What is a magnetic field?**

This experiment proves that magnetism passe[s] through non-magnetic materials, while magnetic ma[-]terials gather the lines of magnetic force and ver[y] little magnetism, if any, passes beyond.

up to the pole of a magnet and remain there although nothing you can see is holding the paper clip from falling. A magnet can cause a steel spring — an elastic object — to bend, stretch, or be compressed. Since magnetism can do all the things that show a force is acting, magnetism must be one kind of force. The area in which lines of magnetic force act is called a *magnetic field*.

To do this experiment, you must use an alnico magnet, because other magnets prob-ably will not be strong enough. If you use a bar magnet, build a pile of books about ten inches high. Place the magnet on the books, so that one pole of the magnet projects over the edge of the pile.

**Can magnetism pass through materials?**

If you use a horseshoe magnet, build two piles of books, each about 15 inches high and ten inches apart. Place a one-foot ruler or a stick the same length across the space between the books. Tie the magnet to the middle of the ruler with a short piece of string, so that the poles hang downward.

Tie a 15-inch piece of string to a paper clip. Push a thumbtack part way into a piece of wood. Wind the thread twice around the thumbtack about five inches from the loose end of the thread. With one hand, hold the paper clip ¼ of an inch away from the magnet. With the other hand, gently pull the loose end of the thread until it is tight. Then push the thumbtack all the way into the wood, securing the thread tightly to the wood. Let go of the paper clip. It will remain suspended in the air, pointing at the magnet.

Carefully, without touching the paper clip, pass between the magnet and the paper clip the following materials: a piece of paper, a piece of cardboard, the corner of an aluminum cookie tin, a piece of plastic sandwich wrapping, a thin flat piece of glass, a silver coin, a penny, a wide rubber band. If you did all this carefully, the paper clip remained suspended in the air while the magnet continued to attract it. This means that magnetism had to pass through each of the materials you placed between the magnet and paper clip. In this experiment you have learned that magnetism can pass through several different kinds of materials. What do all these materials have in common? They all are non-magnetic materials.

Now, pass a penknife blade between the paper clip and the magnet. The paper clip falls down. Put the paper clip back into its suspended position.

Cut one end out of a tin can with a can opener. Slip this piece of metal between the paper clip and the magnet. Again, the paper clip falls. Try this once again, using a large nail in place of the knife blade. When the nail is between the paper clip and the magnet, the paper clip will fall. Why does the paper clip fall when the knife blade, the end of the tin can, and the nail are placed between it and the magnet? The answer must be that magnetism cannot pass through these things. What do they have in common? All of them are made of iron or steel, magnetic materials. (A tin can is made of steel thinly coated with tin.) Magnetism easily passes into a magnetic material, which gathers together the lines of magnetic force, so that little, if any, magnetism passes beyond. Suppose that water is magnetism and a stretched-out handkerchief is a sheet of non-magnetic material. If you pour

some water on the handkerchief, the water will flow right through, just as magnetism passes through a non-magnetic material. Now, suppose that a large sponge is a magnetic material. If you pour some water on the sponge, the water will be absorbed into the sponge and none will pass through, just as magnetism is absorbed and does not pass through a magnetic material.

Let us prove in another way what we have just learned. Cut two strips of cardboard two inches wide and about a foot long. Make two piles of books three inches apart. Place the two cardboard strips, one on top of the other, and put both on top of the books. Place more books on each pile. Put a magnet on top of the cardboard strips. Place some tacks (or paper clips) against the bottom of the cardboard, just under the magnet. The tacks will be held up by the magnet.

Slip a knife blade between the two strips of cardboard, just below the magnet. The tacks will fall. Try this experiment again, using the end of the tin can.

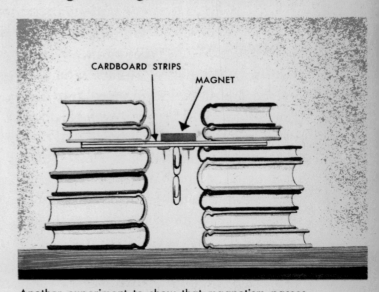

Another experiment to show that magnetism passes through non-magnetic materials.

Again, the tacks fall, as the steel absorbs the magnetic force.

Perhaps, when you bought your horseshoe magnet it had a piece of metal across its poles. If you bought a pair of bar magnets, perhaps they had a piece of metal bridging the two bars at each end. These pieces of metal are called *armatures,* or *keepers.* They are made of a very magnetic metal and ab-

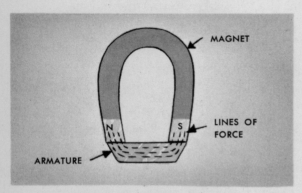

Armatures absorb lines of magnetic force and by doing so preserve the magnet's strength.

sorb the lines of magnetic force. This helps to preserve the strength of the magnet.

You may have seen a watch advertised to be non-magnetic.

**What is a non-magnetic watch?** This means that the working parts of the watch will not be affected by magnetism. People working near large electric motors or other kinds of electrical or electronic machines need non-magnetic watches. There are strong magnetic fields around such machinery, and the magnetic lines of force, affecting the springs of the watch, can prevent it from keeping correct time. However, if the working parts of the watch are enclosed in a case made of a material that is a very good magnetic absorber, magnetic

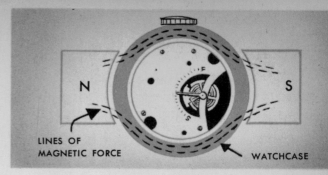

The lines of magnetic force will not reach the spring; they are absorbed by the watch case.

lines of force will be absorbed and held by the watchcase and will not reach the springs of the watch. But this way of making a watch non-magnetic is awkward because a large, thick watch-case is needed.

A new and better way of making a non-magnetic watch has recently been made possible. A non-magnetic steel alloy has been found that can be used to make watch springs. Thus, all the parts of the watch can be made of non-magnetic metals. Magnetism passes entirely through such watches and cannot affect their timekeeping at all.

If you were to break a bar magnet in halves, wouldn't **What is the smallest magnet?** you expect to have one half with a north pole and the other half with a south pole? Yet, if you were to test the

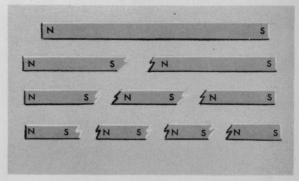

By breaking a magnet in parts, you get little magnets, each one having its own north and south pole.

two halves, you would find that you have two complete magnets, both with north and south poles. If you broke the halves into quarters, and the quarters into eighths, and so on, until you had very small pieces, you would find that each piece is a complete magnet with both a north and a south pole. This fact led the German scientist, Wilhelm Weber, to surmise, a century ago, that each atom of a piece of magnetic material is a magnet, with a north and a south pole of its own. You probably know that all forms of matter are made up of extremely small particles called atoms. Each atom is made up of a central nucleus around which revolve electrically-charged particles called electrons.

Weber's guess was a brilliant one; modern physicists have learned that, as an electron revolves around the nucleus, it spins on its axis and, because of this spin, generates a magnetic field. Thus, an electron is the smallest known magnet.

The magnetic properties of materials are due to the way the atoms of these materials have their electrons' magnetic fields lined up. Magnetic materials have groups of atoms whose magnetic fields are more or less permanently lined up.

These groups of atoms are called *magnetic domains*. In an unmagnetized piece of magnetic material, the domains are arranged in a haphazard manner. As a magnetic material becomes more and more magnetized, more and more of its magnetic domains line up, with their north poles all pointing in one direction and their south poles in the opposite direction. When the majority of its domains have been lined up, a material is magnetized.

Now that we know what causes a material to be magnetic, let us see whether we can find ways to make a magnet. We have to find ways to line up the atoms in the majority of the magnetic domains.

**How can you make a magnet?**

Pick up a paper clip with a magnet. Touch another paper clip to the end of the one the magnet is holding. The second paper clip is held to the first. See how many paper clips your magnet will hold in a chain. Each paper clip in the chain must act as a magnet in order to hold the one below it. This means that simply by touching the paper clip to a pole of the magnet, the magnetic domains in the paper clip are lined up, and

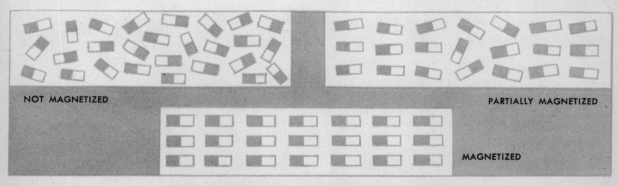

NOT MAGNETIZED

PARTIALLY MAGNETIZED

MAGNETIZED

The illustration shows schematically how atoms are arranged in an unmagnetized bar magnet, in one that is partially magnetized, and in one that is completely magnetized.

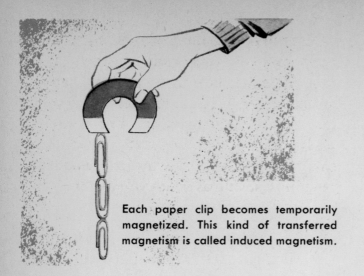

Each paper clip becomes temporarily magnetized. This kind of transferred magnetism is called induced magnetism.

the paper clip becomes magnetized. Magnetism transferred in this way from magnetized material to unmagnetized material is called *induced magnetism*.

If you can obtain a steel bar about two feet long and half an inch in diameter, you can magnetize the bar in a simple way. Hold the bar so that it points in the direction that a compass needle points. Holding the bar in this position, strike the end of it hard 20 times with a hammer. Now, see whether the ends of the bar will pick up iron filings or paper clips. They will, and you have made a magnet. Pointing the bar north lined it up parallel to the field of

the largest magnet we have — the earth itself. Striking the bar helped to disturb the atoms in their magnetic domains, so that the magnetic field of the earth could line them up with their north poles pointing in one direction and their south poles in the other.

Make a chain of paper clips, as you **What is a** did when learning about **permanent** induced magnetism. Pull **magnet?** the uppermost paper clip away from the magnet. The chain falls apart. Try to pick up one paper clip with another; it cannot be done, because none of the paper clips are magnetized any longer.

Let us try harder to make a paper clip into a magnet. Stroke the paper clip across one pole of a magnet. Do not stroke the paper clip back and forth; stroke it in one direction only, lifting it off the magnet when you come to one end and putting the other end back on the magnet. When you have completed 20 strokes, see whether the paper clip will pick up other paper clips. It will not. This means that it cannot retain the

Striking the steel bar with a hammer helps to disturb the atoms in their magnetic domains enough to line them up with the earth's magnetic field.

GEOGRAPHIC NORTH POLE

INDUCED NORTH POLE

magnetism induced in it by the magnet. In both these experiments, you may find that a small amount of magnetism *does* remain in the paper clips. This little bit of left-over magnetism is called *residual magnetism*. It will gradually disappear with the passing of time.

Clearly, the magnetism induced in the paper clips is temporary. Magnets that lose all, or almost all, of their magnetism when they are no longer in a magnetic field are called *temporary magnets*. The atoms of the magnetic domains of materials that make temporary magnets are easily lined up, even by weak magnetic fields, but they just as easily lose their alignment when removed from the magnetic field.

Obtain a large sewing needle. Stroke the needle several times across one pole of a magnet. Stroke the needle just as you did the paper clip, not back and forth, but in one direction only, lifting it off the magnet when you come to one end, and putting the other end back on the magnet. When you have done this about 20 times, place the magnet out of reach and see whether the needle will pick up a small paper clip or some iron filings. It will. Since the needle is no longer in the magnet's field and yet remains magnetized, you can see that the atoms of the needle's magnetic domains must remain lined up after they are removed from the magnetic field. If you put the needle away and test it again tomorrow or a week or a month from now, you will find that it is still magnetized. Magnets made from materials that remain magnetized after being removed from a magnetic field are called *permanent magnets*.

A remarkable thing about inducing temporary or permanent magnets is that, no matter how many new magnets are made, the original magnet does not lose any of its magnetism. You could magnetize millions of needles from a small magnet and the magnet would remain as strong as when you began.

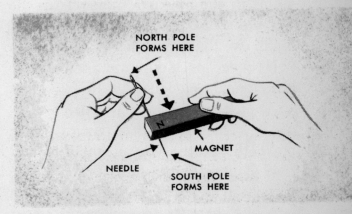

To make a permanent magnet out of a sewing needle, you have to stroke the needle in one direction only with one pole of a magnet.

Permanent magnets have many uses. Placed in a roller at the end of a conveyor belt carrying iron ore and pieces of rock, a permanent magnet holds the iron ore on the belt as it turns over the roller. As a result, the iron ore falls in one pile and the unwanted rock shoots off into another pile. In the same way, stray pieces of iron are separated from coal; but this time, it is the iron that is unwanted. Permanent magnets pick stray pieces of iron out of flour, chemicals, and textiles. A large permanent magnet lowered on the end of a rope is used by police to drag rivers or lakes for guns or other steel objects. A small permanent magnet lowered on the end of a string may be used to retrieve small iron or steel objects dropped into the drain-pipes of sinks.

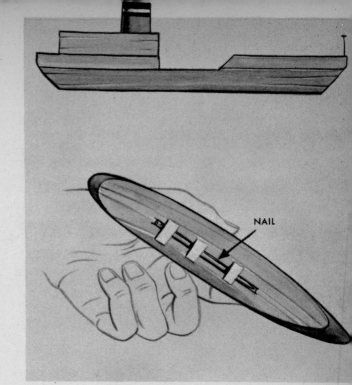

If you have the steel bar you magnetized

**How can you demagnetize a magnet?** by striking its end, hold it so that it runs along an east-west line. Strike the bar several times, on its sides as well as its end. Now test it to see whether it still is magnetic. It is not. By jarring the atoms of the magnetic domains in the bar, you cause them to lose their alignment, so that their north and south poles cancel each other out, and the bar is no longer magnetized.

Another way to demagnetize a magnet is to heat it. With a pair of pliers, grasp the needle you magnetized and hold it in a flame until it is red hot. Place it in an east-west direction and let it cool. Then try to pick up a paper clip with the needle. You will find that the needle has lost its magnetism. The heat caused the atoms of the needle to move about very rapidly and, in doing so, to disarrange themselves.

A heated magnet loses its magnetism at a very definite temperature. This temperature is called the *Curie point,* for its discoverer, Pierre Curie, a French scientist. Each magnetic material has its own Curie point. For iron it is about 800° Centigrade; for nickel, about 350° Centigrade.

When we say that a demagnetized material has lost its magnetism, we do not mean that the magnetism has gone out of the material or that the magne-

Heat can demagnetize a magnet.

tism has been destroyed. Each atom and each electron is just as much a magnet as when the material was magnetized, but the tiny magnets are no longer lined up so as to produce one big magnet.

Now that you know jarring and heating will result in demagnetizing, you should avoid dropping, pounding, or heating your magnets.

Use a toy boat, or whittle one out of a

**How can you make a magnetic boat?** piece of wood. Cut the head off an iron nail or use a headless nail, the kind called a "finishing nail." If you are using a wooden boat, cut a short slot in its bottom. The slot should be just big enough for the nail to fit into it. If the nail fits the slot snugly, you will not have to do anything more to keep it in place. If the nail does not fit tightly into the slot, or if you are using a boat into which you cannot cut a slot, attach the nail to the bottom of the boat with waterproof

22

## THE BOAT WITH THE "MAGNETIC MOTOR"

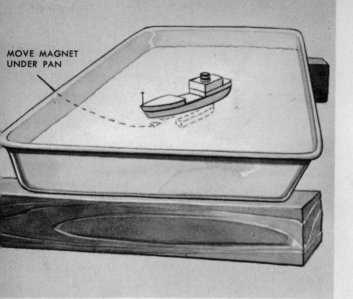

MOVE MAGNET
UNDER PAN

cement or with strips of adhesive tape such as doctors use when bandaging.

Using bricks or blocks of wood, prop up an aluminum pan or a wooden or china bowl so that you can move your hand around beneath it. The pan or bowl should be large enough, when filled with water, to float your boat in it. When you have floated the boat, move a magnet around on the underside of the pan. You will be able to make the boat sail wherever you wish.

Instead of a boat, you might use a toy fish or whittle one out of wood. Your magnetic fish will swim wherever you make it go with your magnet.

# The Earth as a Magnet

The earth is a huge magnet. It possesses a magnetic field around it as though a powerful bar magnet were embedded in its center. Of course, there is no bar magnet in the center of the earth. Scientists believe that the main source of the earth's magnetism is within the cores of the earth. These cores are probably made of a combination of iron and nickel. They are under tremendous pressure and are very hot. The inner core, a sphere 1,600 miles in diameter, is probably solid. The outer core, 1,400 miles thick and 1,800 miles beneath the earth's surface, surrounds the inner core. The outer core is probably like a very stiff paste. Slow movements of the inner core within the outer core, and movements within the outer core itself, produce the earth's main magnetic field.

A second, much weaker, magnetic

**What is geomagnetism?**

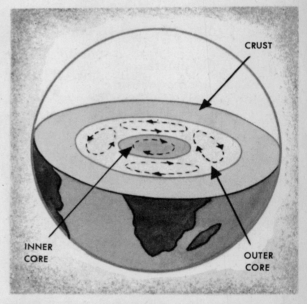

CRUST

INNER CORE

OUTER CORE

Scientists believe that the main source of the earth's magnetism is within the cores of the earth.

field is generated by the earth's ionosphere (eye-on'-o-sveer), a layer of air 60 to 100 miles above the earth's surface. The ionosphere is made up of electrically charged particles. As these particles move about in great wind-like

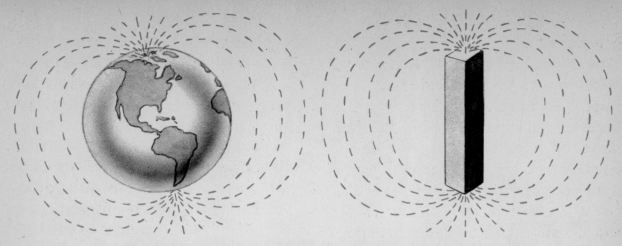

The earth has a magnetic field of force just as a bar magnet does.

gusts, a magnetic field is generated. Although scientists can separate the two magnetic fields, for all practical purposes we can say that the earth has just one great magnetic field. The earth's magnetism is called *geomagnetism; geo* means "earth."

It is very important not to confuse the

**What is the difference between geomagnetism and gravity?**

earth's magnetism with its gravity. You know that an unsupported object, whether it is a ball that you throw into the air, or a space ship circling the earth, or an X-15 rocket plane, falls toward the earth's surface. When we say that it "falls," we mean that it is pulled toward the earth by the force of gravity. This pull of gravity seems very much like the attraction a magnet has for magnetic materials. Scientists know even less about gravity than about magnetism, but they can see some differences between these two natural forces. A magnet will attract only magnetic materials but gravity exerts its pull on all objects, no matter of what material they are made. No object has been found to

have "gravitational poles" such as a magnetized object's magnetic poles. The earth's magnetic pull is weak compared to its gravitational pull. You have to work hard against the pull of gravity to pick up most objects even half as big as you are, but you could pick up an iron object at one of the earth's magnetic poles without even being able to notice the magnetic pull added to the weight of the object. A small steel magnet has a magnetic field about 10 times as strong as the earth's magnetic field, and an alnico magnet's field is almost 100 times as strong.

When you learned that the north pole

**Why is a magnet's north pole really a south pole?**

of a magnet is the north-pointing pole, did you wonder why one pole of a magnet always points north? You know that opposite magnetic poles attract; might it not be that the north pole of a magnet is *attracted* northward? That is exactly what happens. The north-pointing pole of a magnet is attracted northward by a huge magnet — the earth, itself.

Oddly, then, the north-pointing pole

of a magnet must really be a south pole! This is true because unlike magnetic poles attract. So, the south pole of a magnet is attracted northward by the north magnetic pole of the earth. This means that the north pole, or north-pointing pole, of a magnet is really a south pole. However, the north-pointing pole of a magnet is called the north pole, and you must think of it as a north pole when you work with magnets.

A compass needle is simply a thin magnet balanced on a pivot in a manner that permits the magnet to turn easily. As a result, the earth's north magnetic pole attracts one end of the compass needle, so that it always points north. Probably because the earliest use of a magnet as a compass took place in the northern hemisphere, we talk about a compass needle always pointing north. We could just as correctly pay attention to the other pole, the south pole of the

**What is a compass?**

magnetic needle, and say that a compass always points south. The more scientific way of describing how a compass needle acts is to say that it points along a north-south line.

A woodsman's compass, or scouting compass, looks something like a pocket watch. The dial of the compass has the four geographical directions printed on it: north (N), south (S), east (E), and west (W). These four directions are called the *cardinal points* of the compass. Usually, printed between the cardinal points are at least four other compass points: northeast (NE), southeast (SE), southwest (SW), and northwest (NW). The compass needle rests on a pivot raised up from the center of the dial. The dial and needle are contained in a metal case covered by glass to keep out dust.

Suppose you are lost in the woods on a cloudy day. You cannot use the sun

**How do you use a compass?**

MAGNETIC POLE

GEOGRAPHIC NORTH POLE

MAGNETIC POLE

GEOGRAPHIC SOUTH POLE

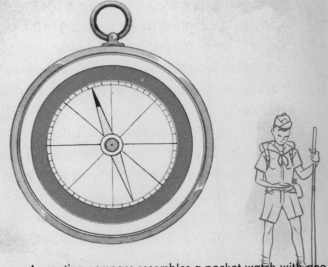

A scouting compass resembles a pocket watch with geographical directions instead of numbers on the dial.

The north-pointing pole of a magnet is really a south pole, and the south-pointing pole a north pole.

to guide you, and you know that if you walk in the direction that you think is home, you will probably walk in circles, as do most people lost in the woods. You must depend on your compass to guide you safely home.

Let's say you know that if you walk due west, you will come to a landmark, perhaps a road or a river or stream, that will lead you home. You place your compass on a flat rock, a tree stump, or some other level surface. When the compass needle stops swinging, you know that it is pointing north. Looking at the dial, you find that the part of the dial beneath the north pole of the needle probably does not read N, or north. To remedy this, you carefully turn the compass, keeping the needle as still as possible, until the N on the compass dial is directly beneath the north-pointing arm of the needle. As a result, the N on the dial faces north, S south, E east, and W west.

You pick up the compass and walk in the direction of the W on the dial, meanwhile keeping the north-pointing arm of the compass needle over the N on the dial. Every once in a while, you set the compass down on a level surface in order to make sure that the needle has not been turned away by tilting when you walked. As long as you follow the direction in which the W points, you will be walking west, and soon you will come to the landmark that will lead you home.

A mariner's compass is one in which

**How does a mariner use a compass to guide his ship?**

a circular card rests on the magnet. On the card are printed 32 compass points and 360 equal divisions, or degrees. Every apprentice seaman must learn to recite all 32 compass points in correct order, beginning with north and going clockwise around the dial. Doing this is called "boxing the compass." The circular card is attached to the magnet so that the north pole of the magnet is directly beneath the N mark on the card. Thus, when the compass needle points north, the N on the card points north.

At the rim of the mariner's compass there is a mark that is in a straight line with the bow, or front, of the ship. When the helmsman steers the ship so that the N on the dial card points directly to this mark, then the ship is sailing north. If he wants to sail northwest, he turns the ship so that NW on the dial points directly to the mark.

The magnetic pole of the earth's northern hemisphere is

**What is magnetic declination?**

not located at the North Pole, but at 76° north latitude and 102° west longitude. This is a point approximately 2,000 miles due north of Bismarck, North Dakota, and 1,000 miles south of the north pole. The south magnetic pole is at a point about 2,300 miles due south of Melbourne, Australia.

It was not long after mariners began to use compasses that they realized the compass needle does not point directly north. We know that this is so because the north magnetic pole and the north geographic pole are not located at the same point. Mariners learned that in order to know how to sail due north when they were in any part of the world's seas, they had to know just how far away from geographic north their

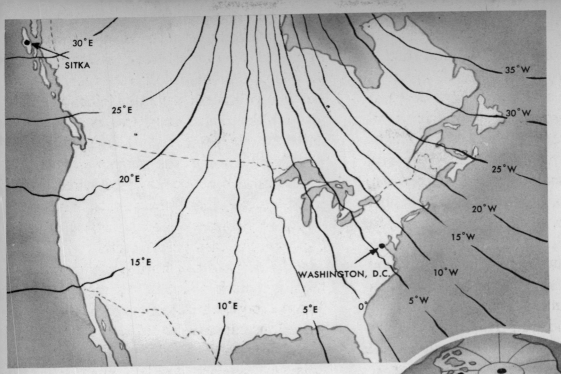

Typical distribution of magnetic declination in the United States.

Geographic north and south poles and magnetic north and south poles are not at identical spots.

compass was pointing. They measured the angle between geographic north and magnetic north. They called this difference the *angle of magnetic declination.* For example, at Washington, D. C., the angle of magnetic declination between true north and magnetic north is 6° W, and in Sitka, Alaska, 30° E. This means that at Washington, D. C., geographic north is 6° to the west of where the north pole of a compass points; in Sitka, north is 30° east of north on the compass.

The earth's magnetic poles are con-

**How do we know that the earth's magnetic poles wander?**

stantly moving about. The movement is slow, but scientists can easily measure it. In 1955, United States government scientists carefully determined the location of the north magnetic pole. Five years later, they repeated the measurements to locate the pole and found that it had moved approximately 70 miles toward the northwest. In the past hundreds of millions of years, the north and south magnetic poles have made distant wanderings about the earth. There were times in the past when the north magnetic pole was in Korea, in the middle of the north Atlantic Ocean, and possibly even in Africa. What is even more remarkable, the north and south magnetic poles seem to have changed places! In fact, this change seems to have taken place about once every million years. No one knows why this happened.

How do scientists know that the

earth's magnetic poles have wandered? Scientists have found natural "compass needles" that tell them where the magnetic poles were in the past. These compass needles are grains of magnetite, or loadstone. There are grains of this mineral in the lava that flows out of volcanoes. When the rock is very hot, the grains are not magnetized, because, as we learned, high temperature demagnetizes magnetic materials. However, as the lava cools, the grains of magnetite reach their Curie point (the temperature at which magnetism is destroyed and at which it reappears, upon cooling) before the lava has hardened to rock. When the grains reach their Curie point, the earth's magnetic field lines them up in a north-south direction. The lava then hardens, and the magnetic grains can no longer move around. But the earth's magnetic field continues to wander. Millions of years later, when scientists examine the rock formed from the lava, they find frozen into the rock thousands of "compass needles" that point to where the north and south magnetic poles were when the rock was formed.

Many kinds of rock form from sediments carried to oceans and lakes by rivers and streams. In the course of millions of years, the grains of sediment are turned into sedimentary rocks by great pressure within the earth. Some of the grains of the future sedimentary rock are grains of magnetite. As these grains are carried along by the water, they are free to turn along a north-south line under the influence of the earth's magnetic poles. When the grains of sediment have become sedimentary rock, the rock contains tiny "compass

needles." From them, future scientists can tell the location of the earth's magnetic poles when the rocks formed.

The earth's magnetic field is not only stronger at the magnetic poles, but also varies slightly from place to place on the surface of the earth. This is due to the presence in the earth of magnetic materials such as bodies of iron, nickel, or cobalt ore. Prospectors found that if they could measure the changes in the earth's magnetic field, they could tell where to mine for valuable metal ores. At first, making a magnetic survey of an area was very slow, because the instruments that made the measurements had to be carried from place to place, sometimes over very rugged country. But today, a very sensitive measuring instrument, called a *magnetometer,* is placed in a bomb-

**How do prospectors use magnetism to find ore?**

surface of the earth along lines of magnetic force. Many of these particles collide with air molecules causing the molecules to vibrate and give off the white, red, blue, and green lights that make up the awesome displays of the auroras. The auroras are seen only in the higher latitudes because the earth's magnetic field is strongest at the north and south magnetic poles.

Not long after the United States began

**What is the Van Allen magnetosphere?**

to put satellites into orbit, scientists found that the earth was surrounded by a huge swarm of radioactive, electrically-charged atomic particles extending 50,000 miles out into space. Just where all these hundreds of billions of radioactive particles come from is not known, but large numbers do come from the sun and are trapped by the earth's magnetic field. At first, scientists thought that there were two great belts of radiation surrounding the earth, a small inner belt, a space without

shaped casing and is towed at the end of a long cable beneath an airplane. Magnetometers are so sensitive that they can detect the presence of a handful of nails on the ground 1500 feet below the airplane.

If you live in the northern part of the

**What causes the aurora borealis, or northern lights?**

United States or in Canada, or in the southern part of the southern hemisphere, you probably have seen great curtains and streamers of light sweeping through the sky at night, especially during the early spring and fall. These lights are the *aurora borealis*, or northern lights. In the southern hemisphere these lights are called the *aurora australis*, or southern lights.

The sun is continually sending out streams of electrically-charged particles. When these particles reach the earth's magnetic field, they spiral toward the

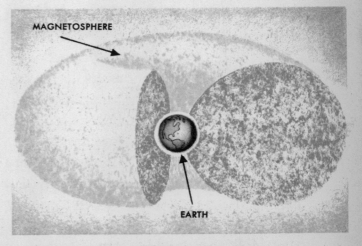

The Van Allen radiation magnetosphere.

radioactive particles, and a vast outer belt. Later, scientists learned that their satellites had not covered all the area in which the particles exist. When exploring satellites had covered the whole area, scientists learned that there is only one great swarm of radioactive particles, very dense near the earth and becoming thinner until it ends 50,000 miles out in space. The single swarm was then named the *magnetosphere*. The presence of the radioactive particles was first discovered by the American physicist, James Van Allen, and the magnetosphere is named for him.

The Van Allen magnetosphere resembles a doughnut that is thickest above the earth's equator where the earth's magnetic field is the weakest. The magnetosphere is quite thin in the northern and southern latitudes near the magnetic poles, where the earth's magnetic field is the strongest. The reason for this is that the electrically-charged particles have magnetic fields. As they arrive from the sun and begin

to cross the earth's magnetic field, they are pushed and pulled sideways. Which way they move depends on the direction that their magnetic poles face in relation to the earth's magnetic poles. Since most of the particles are spinning, they are alternately attracted and repelled, and, therefore, they spiral back and forth along the earth's lines of magnetic force. (Some particles move fast enough to break through the lines of magnetic force and reach the earth's atmosphere or even the earth's surface.) The particles that approach the earth parallel to the north and south magnetic poles do not have to cross lines of magnetic force and are pulled straight into the earth's atmosphere by the very powerful attraction of the earth's magnetic poles. This is why the Van Allen magnetosphere is thinnest near the poles.

Space explorers will have to find ways to shield themselves from the radioactive particles of the Van Allen magnetosphere, because these particles can endanger the lives of astronauts.

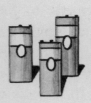 # Electromagnetism

For more than 200 years scientists had

**How did Oersted discover electromagnetism?**

suspected that there was a connection between electricity and magnetism. It was not until 1820 that Hans Christian Oersted, a Danish scientist, proved the connection. One day, Oersted, who was a professor of physics,

accidently placed a compass near a wire carrying an electric current. The compass needle had been parallel to the wire. To Oersted's surprise, the compass needle turned away from its north-south line and pointed crosswise to the wire. Oersted tried this several times and found that the compass needle moved only when current was flowing through the wire. He then understood that a wire carrying a current has a magnetic field around it.

To do this experiment and others that

**How can you perform Oersted's experiment?**

follow, it is best to use an electric switch. You can buy an inexpensive one in a hardware store, but it is much more fun to make one.

Using a pair of tin-shears, cut from a tin can a strip of metal about three inches long and half an inch wide. Be careful not to cut yourself on the sharp edges of the tin! Obtain a piece of wood about the size of a small book. Scrape the insulation off the ends of a piece of wire six inches long. Twist one end of the wire around a small nail near its head. Use this nail to attach one end of the tin strip to the piece of wood. Make sure that you hammer the nail all the way down, so that the wire around it presses the tin firmly to the wood. Bend the piece of tin into two angles, as shown in the illustration on page 23.

Make a mark on the wood under, and ¼ of an inch before, the free end of the tin strip. Turn the strip of tin aside. Hammer a nail into the mark you made on the wood until only half an inch of the nail remains out of the wood. Return the tin strip to its original position. When you push down on the end of the strip, it should touch the head of the nail beneath it. Now you have made a switch. (Never use this switch with any source of electricity other than a dry-cell battery. If you do, you will receive a painful shock, or even kill yourself!)

To do Oersted's experiment, you need a compass, a dry-cell battery, and some wire. You can probably buy all three in a five-and-ten-cent store, and certainly in a hardware store. The kind of wire called "bell wire" is best.

Scrape the insulation off both ends of a piece of wire about two feet long. Twist one end of this wire around the nail beneath the end of the tin strip. Attach the other end of wire to the center binding post of the dry cell. Scrape the insulation off both ends of a piece of wire three feet long. Attach one end of this wire to the other binding post of the dry cell, and twist the other end together with the free end of the wire that you nailed to the board.

Place a compass near your switch. Hold a portion of the long wire across the face of the compass. Make sure the north-seeking pole of the compass needle points to the N on the face of the compass and parallel to the wire. Now, push down on your switch to close the electric circuit and make electricity flow from the battery through the wires. What happens to the compass needle? It turns crosswise to the wire. Release the switch. The needle swings back to its normal north-south line. Push and release the switch a few more times. You will see that it is only when electric current is flowing through the wire that the needle swings crosswise to the wire. This proves a current flowing through a wire sets up a magnetic field around the wire (see page 33).

Disconnect the two wires from the binding posts of the battery. Switch them around, that is, connect the long wire to the center binding post and the shorter wire to the other binding post. This change will make the current in the wire flow in the opposite direction. Hold the wire across the compass, as before, and push the switch. This time, the compass needle swings in the opposite direction from that which it did when the wires were connected the other way. This shows that a change in the direction of the current in the wire reverses the direction of the poles of the magnetic field set up around the wire.

We have learned that a current-carrying wire produces a magnetic field around itself. Might

**What is an electromagnet?**

not this fact be used to make some kind of magnet? Yes, an *electromagnet*. An electromagnet consists of a bar of magnetic material around which are wound many turns of wire. When an electric current is sent through the wire, the lines of magnetic force produced by the current are concentrated in the bar. The bars of electromagnets are usually made of soft iron or any alloy that is easily magnetized and, therefore, easily demagnetized. When the current stops running through the wire, the bar loses practically all its magnetism immediately. In the opening sentence of this book, we read about a large magnet that picked up scrap iron and steel in a junk yard. This kind of magnet is an electromagnet. You can see that if an electromagnet did not lose its magnetism when the current is turned off, the junkyard magnet could not drop the objects that it picks up; they would stick to it until someone pulled them off. Such a magnet would be hard to use.

Obtain a bolt about three inches long and a nut to fit on the bolt.

**How can you make an electromagnet?**

Screw the nut on the bolt only far enough so that the bottom of the bolt just begins to protrude from the nut. Beginning a foot from the end of a long piece of bell wire, wind the wire around the bolt, starting at the head of the bolt and working toward the nut. Each turn of the wire should touch the one before it. Cover the length of the bolt with two or three layers of wire, making sure that, as you wind back and forth, you continue to wind in the same direction. Leave a foot of wire when you reach the last turn. To secure the wire, slip its end under the last turn. Scrape the insulation off the free ends of the wire, and twist one end around the end of the wire that is secured to the switch you made. Attach the other end to a binding post of your dry cell. Now, attach a wire from the nail of your switch to the other binding post of the dry cell. Hold the end of the bolt over a pile of paper clips and push the switch. The bolt has become an electromagnet that picks up the paper clips. Release the switch. The paper clips drop off the bolt. (It is possible that you may have used a hard steel bolt. If you did, you made a permanent magnet of the bolt, and it will continue to hold the paper clips.) You can make a stronger electromagnet by winding more turns of wire about the bolt, or by connecting the electromagnet to more than one dry cell.

Electric current flowing through a wire sets up a magnetic field.

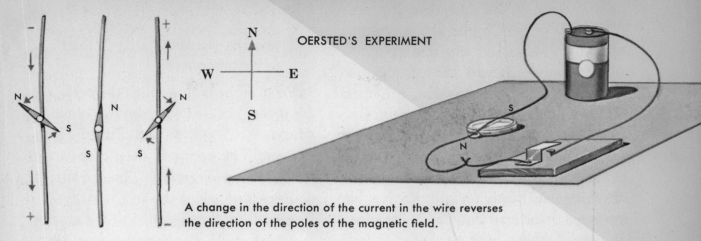

OERSTED'S EXPERIMENT

A change in the direction of the current in the wire reverses the direction of the poles of the magnetic field.

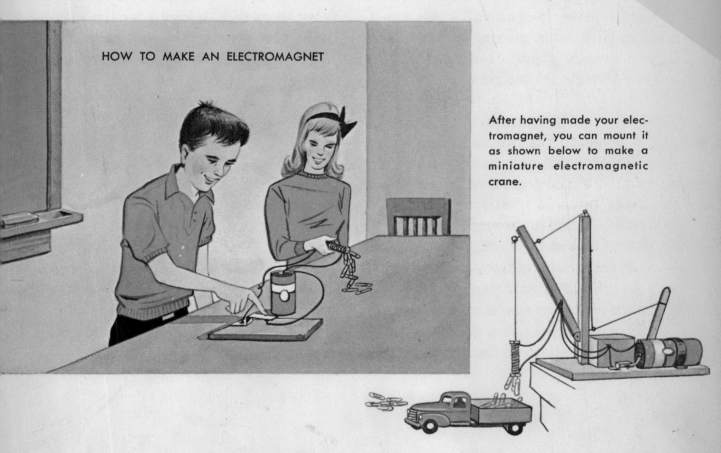

HOW TO MAKE AN ELECTROMAGNET

After having made your electromagnet, you can mount it as shown below to make a miniature electromagnetic crane.

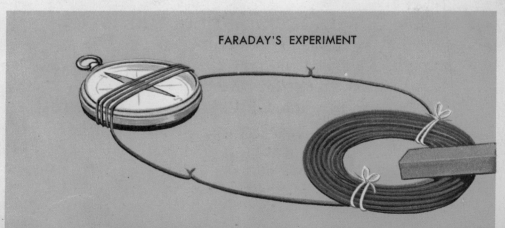

FARADAY'S EXPERIMENT

How to induce electricity by moving a magnet within a coil of wire is described on page 34. When you stop moving the magnet, no electricity will be induced.

If a current flowing through a wire can produce a magnetic field, might not a wire moving through a magnetic field produce a current? The British physicist, Michael Faraday, pondered this question for years and performed many experiments without success. Finally, in 1820, by accident, he found that when he poked a bar magnet through a coil of wire, he produced an electric current in the wire. He then found that it made no difference whether he moved the magnet through the coil of wire or the coil of wire over the magnet. Both actions produced an electric current.

**How can a magnet produce electricity?**

Wind about 20 turns of bell wire around a paper cup, beginning a foot from the end of the wire. Collapse the cup, leaving a coil of wire. Tie the wires of the coil together with pieces of string at opposite sides of the coil. Wind about four turns of bell wire around a compass so that the wire passes over the face of the compass. Connect the ends of this wire to the ends of the wire from the

**How can you do Faraday's experiment?**

coil. When a current flows in the wire, a magnetic field will be produced and the compass needle will move. (See page 33 for illustration of the experiment.)

Poke a bar magnet into the coil. The compass needle will move. Note in which direction it moved. Pull the magnet out. The compass needle moves in the opposite direction. This means, of course, that when the magnet reverses its direction, the direction of the current is reversed. Hold the magnet still and move the coil. The results are the same as if you moved the magnet.

Try stopping the movement of the magnet at different parts of the coil. As soon as the motion stops, the compass needle stops moving, indicating that the current has stopped flowing. Therefore, we can guess that it is motion of a wire through a magnetic field that produces an electric current. This guess is right. From this experiment we learn that we need three things to generate electricity in this manner: we need a magnet, a conductor such as wire through which the electric current flows, and motion. If any of these things is lacking, no electricity will be generated.

# Electromagnets In Use

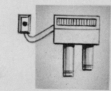

An electric bell, like the one that rings when someone pushes the button outside your front door, uses an electromagnet. The push-button is a switch. When it is pushed,

**How does a doorbell work?**

electric current flows into the coils of the electromagnet on the bell, and a metal strip called the *armature* is pulled toward the magnet. At the top of the metal strip is a knob that strikes the bell.

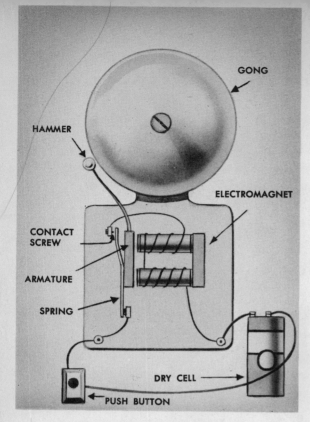

The working parts of an electric bell.

electromagnet no longer pulls on the armature. The brass strip springs back, pulling the armature with it and touching the contact screw again. The circuit is established once more, and the whole sequence of events repeats itself as long as you push on the button.

A buzzer works exactly like a bell, but it makes a buzzing sound instead of a musical sound because in a buzzer, the knob strikes a solid object, instead of a hollow bell.

### What is a dynamo?

We learned that moving a conductor (the coil of wire) through a magnetic field produces an electric current. In 1832, the French inventor

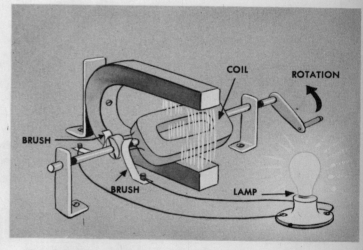

The dynamo changes mechanical energy into electrical energy by electromagnetic induction.

It is reasonable to think that once you push the switch and close the circuit, the armature will be pulled toward the electromagnet and remain there until you release the switch. But you know that this is not what happens when you push the button of a doorbell. Instead, as long as you hold your finger on the button, the armature leaps rapidly back and forth, banging the knob on the bell. How does this happen? The armature is attached to a springy strip of brass that is in contact with a pointed screw, called the *contact screw*. The electric current enters the electromagnet through the contact screw. As soon as the electromagnet pulls the armature, the attached strip of brass also is pulled toward the electromagnet and away from the contact screw, breaking the circuit. When this happens, there is no electric current in the circuit, and the

Hyppolyte Pixii made use of this fact to invent the first device for generating a steady electric current. He made the first electric generator, or *dynamo*. When the coil is turned around within the magnetic field, electric current is generated in the wires that make up the coil. The current flows into the axle and through the contacts to the conductors which are wires. The wires can lead to an electrical appliance, such as a light bulb, an electric iron, a radio, or dozens of other devices that are powered by electricity.

In a modern electric generating plant, such as the one that supplies electricity to your home, there may be one or more huge dynamos having magnets ten feet high and armatures containing tens of thousands of turns of wire. The armatures are turned in the magnetic field by turbines powered by steam or by water falling from a dam.

Below, the working parts of a simple D.C. motor.

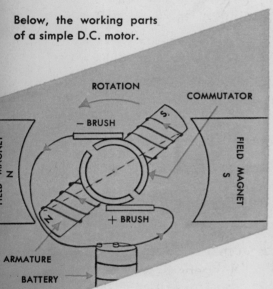

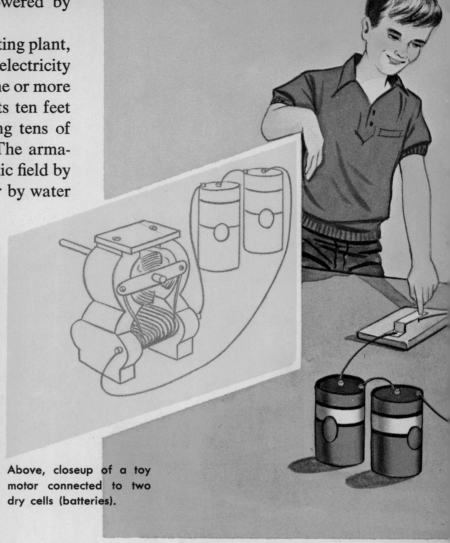

Above, closeup of a toy motor connected to two dry cells (batteries).

**How does an electric motor use magnets?** We have learned that like magnetic poles repel, and unlike poles attract, each other. This Law of Magnetic Poles is the principle behind an electric motor. An electric motor consists of one magnet turning inside another due to their poles alternately attracting and repelling one another.

Suspend a magnet as you did when learning the Law of Magnetic Poles. Bring the N pole of another magnet near the N pole of the suspended mag-

net. The N pole of the suspended magnet will, of course, swing away from the approaching N pole of the magnet in your hand. As soon as the N pole of the suspended magnet has made a quarter turn, bring the N pole of the magnet in your hand near the approaching S pole of the suspended magnet. Doing this will attract the swinging S pole. Pull the magnet in your hand out of the way, and as the S pole swings past, turn the magnet in your hand so that its S pole gives the swinging S pole a push. By alternately pushing and pull-

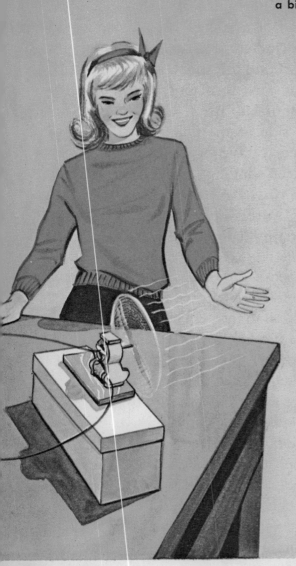

When the wire is the coil of an electromagnet, reversing the direction of the current reverses the electromagnet's poles.

The magnet that forms the outer part of an electric motor is stationary. This magnet, called the *field magnet,* may be an electromagnet or a permanent magnet, but its poles do not change. The second magnet, called the *armature,* is located between the poles of the field magnet. The armature, attached to a rod that enables it to spin around, has a coil of wire wound around it. When current enters the wires of the coil, the armature becomes an electromagnet. The like poles of the armature and field magnet repel and the unlike poles attract. As a result the armature turns. When unlike poles come into position near each other, they should stop the armature from turning any farther, if nothing else happens.

Just before the unlike poles face each

ing the poles of the suspended magnet with the magnet in your hand, you can make the suspended magnet revolve quite rapidly. An electric motor works in a similar manner.

At least one magnet in an electric motor must be an electromagnet. This is so because an electromagnet can be made to change its poles when the direction of the electric current is reversed. You remember that Oersted learned that if he changed the direction of the electric current in a wire, it acted like a magnet whose poles are reversed.

A small kitchen mixer and a big electric locomotive are both driven by electric motors.

other, a little device on the armature reverses the direction of the current. This reversing device is called a *commutator*. The reversal of the direction of the current reverses the poles of the armature. Now, the unlike poles that were facing each other are like poles repelling each other. The armature now makes another turn.

As rapidly as the armature spins, the current reverses, and the armature goes on turning as long as current is supplied to the motor. Some armatures turn more than a thousand revolutions a minute.

An electric motor is one of the most useful pieces of machinery we have. We snap a switch, and an electric motor works immediately, powerfully, and quietly. Just think how clumsy it would be to run a kitchen mixer or an air conditioner with a gasoline or steam engine. Electric motors run washers, refrigerators, typewriters, fans, drills, and scores of other useful appliances.

Powerful electric motors have many uses in industry. They run elevators and hoists that lift heavy loads. They move assembly lines. Electric motors run trains, streetcars, and subways.

To make an armature take a brand new round (not hexagonal) pencil and saw off the brass ferule that holds the eraser. Sharpen both ends of the pencil. Obtain a small wooden sewing-thread spool. Saw and whittle square notches out of opposite sides of the spool. Push the pencil through the hole in the spool.

**How can you make an electric motor?**

Wind the armature in the following manner. Beginning about an inch from the end of a coil of No. 22 lacquered wire, wind three layers of wire lengthwise around the spool. Wind it closely, so that each turn touches the turn before and after itself. Cross over to the other side of the pencil to cover both surfaces of the notches. Be sure that you keep winding in the same direction. When you have finished, leave about an inch of wire. Secure this end of the wire by looping it into a simple knot at the end of the last turn.

Beneath the loose ends of the wire, cement two half-inch-wide strips of metal foil to the pencil so that each strip goes almost half way around the pencil, but does not touch on either side. Scrape the lacquer off the ends of the wire. Secure an end of the wire to each piece of metal foil, using adhesive or cellophane tape.

Drill a $\frac{5}{16}$-inch hole part way into a block of wood that is 3½ inches long, 1¾ inches wide, and ¾ inch thick. Cut notches in the block as shown.

Obtain two iron bolts, $\frac{5}{16}$ of an inch

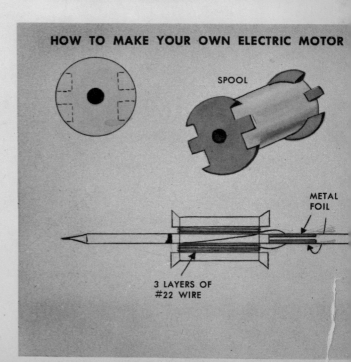

HOW TO MAKE YOUR OWN ELECTRIC MOTOR

SPOOL

METAL FOIL

3 LAYERS OF #22 WIRE

in diameter and about 2½ inches long. Also obtain four metal washers that fit closely around the bolt. Place the washers on the bolt and then screw the bolt tightly into the hole in the block, leaving 1⅜ inches out of the hole. Repeat these steps using a second block of wood and the other bolt.

Starting one foot from the end of a coil of No. 22 lacquered wire, wind the wire closely around the bolt, beginning where the bolt enters the wood. Be sure that one washer is at each end of the bolt. Wind six tight layers of wire on the bolt. When you have finished winding, secure the wire with a simple loop knot. Leaving about 10 inches of wire free, continue winding on the other bolt, again beginning where the bolt enters the wood. However, now wind the wire in the direction opposite to that on the first bolt. Wind the wire twice around the notches in the wooden block and secure it with a simple loop knot. Leave a foot more, and then cut the wire. Lastly, wind around the notches of the first block the one foot piece of wire you left free at the begin-

ning and secure it with a loop knot. The bolts and block make up the stationary electromagnets of your motor.

Obtain two more wooden blocks, this time 3½ inches long, 1 inch wide, and ¾ inch thick. Drill a ⅛-inch hole a short way into each block. Each hole should be exactly as far from an end of a block as the bolt holes were from the ends of the other two blocks.

Using a wide, flat board for a base, affix to it the four blocks, as shown in the illustration. Use small wood screws that go through the base and into the bottoms of the blocks. Be sure that the ends of the bolts rest not more than an eighth of an inch from the armature. Place the pencil points of the armature in the empty holes in the blocks.

Cut from a coat hanger two straight

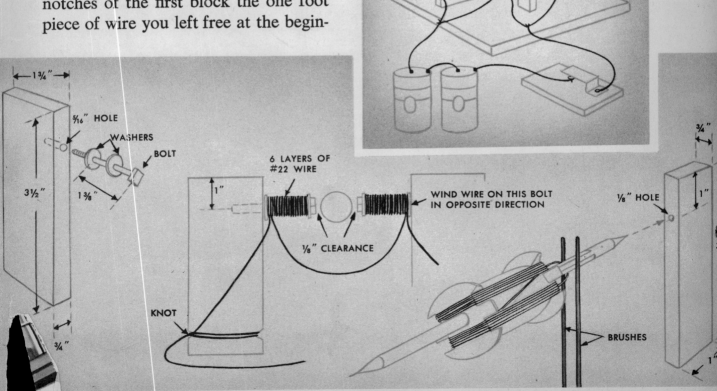

pieces of wire, each 3½ inches long. Place them upright in holes in the wooden base, so that they lightly touch the strips of metal foil on the pencil. The pieces of wire are your motor's brushes.

Connect wires to the brushes. Finally, connect all wires as shown in the illustration. Wherever wires connect, scrape off the lacquer. Two of the wires are run to a pair of dry cells that are connected.

If you have made the motor carefully, when you press down on your switch, the armature of the motor should begin to spin.

Among the most useful tools an atomic scientist has are huge machines called *particle accelerators,* or "atom smashers." These machines use electromagnets to give atomic particles

**What part do magnets play in atomic research?**

speeds almost as fast as light — almost 186,000 miles a second. One very important atom smasher is the *cyclotron.* A cyclotron consists of a large metal box, shaped like a pill box, located between the poles of a huge electromagnet. Air is removed from the box until a very high vacuum exists inside. Within the box there are two hollow, D-shaped half-circles of metal, called *dees.* These are given a very high electric charge that reverses itself millions of times a second. The atomic particles, perhaps protons, are fed into the cyclotron at the center of the dees. The electric charge on the atomic particle affects its magnetic field, and the big electromagnet either repels or attracts the particle. This causes the particle to begin to circle around within the dee. As it passes from one dee to another, the reversing electric charge reverses the charge on the dees. So, a particle that began to move because it was re-

The huge cyclotron at the University of California, Berkeley.

pelled when like magnetic poles acted upon one another, will not be pulled in the opposite direction when it moves into an area of unlike magnetic poles. The reversing electric field allows the particle to always be in a location where it will be repelled. As a result, the particle travels faster and faster in a spiral path until it reaches the outside wall of a dee. Here it shoots out of the cyclotron. The beam of very fast atomic particles shooting out of a cyclotron at targets of various materials enable scientists to learn very much about these materials and the particles that strike them.

# Magnets In Communication

A telegraph is an apparatus for sending messages long distances over wires.

**How are magnets used in a telegraph?**

A telegraph circuit includes a sending key, a receiving sounder, and a source of electricity. The *sending key* is a switch that opens and closes the circuit. The important part of the sending key is a metal rod attached to a piece of springy metal. The rod has a button on one end. When the telegraph operator pushes down on this button, the rod makes contact with a small metal screw below it, and thereby closes an electric circuit. When the operator takes his finger off the button, the rod springs up and breaks the circuit.

The *sounder* has a lightweight magnetic metal bar, called an *armature,* suspended a fraction of an inch above the poles of an electromagnet. One end

**TELEGRAPH**

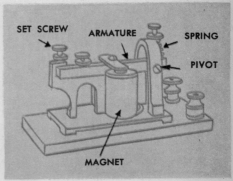

SET SCREW    ARMATURE    SPRING

PIVOT

MAGNET

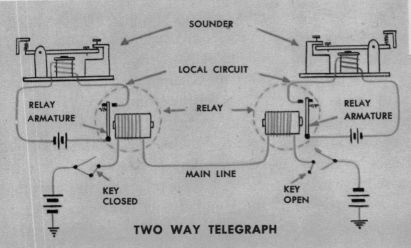

SOUNDER

LOCAL CIRCUIT

RELAY ARMATURE    RELAY    RELAY ARMATURE

MAIN LINE

KEY CLOSED    KEY OPEN

**TWO WAY TELEGRAPH**

At left, the diagram of a two way telegraph line with relays, as described on page 41 and 42.

of the armature is pivoted and has a spring pushing down on the upper part of the pivoted end. The other end is located between a second metal bar and a setscrew. When the telegraph operator pushes the sending key and makes a circuit, the electromagnet pulls one end of the armature suddenly downward. As the armature strikes the bar beneath it, a sharp click is heard. As soon as the operator releases the key, breaking the circuit, the electromagnet releases the end of the armature that it has pulled toward itself; the released end is pushed upward by the spring and strikes the set screw above with another sharp click.

Telegraph operators listen for the time between clicks. A short time (only about 1/5 of a second) is a *dot*. A longer time (about ½ a second) is a *dash*. By means of a code of combinations of dots and dashes, messages are sent along the wire that connects the key to a sounder.

Suppose a telegraph operator in Cincinnati wants to send a message to an operator in Tucson. The Cincinnati operator pushes his telegraph key down. This closes the circuit and electric current flows through the wires, the electromagnet in Tucson works, and the Tucson sounder clicks. You may wonder how electric current can flow through the wires when the telegraph key in Cincinnati is pushed down and the key in Tucson is open and keeping a circuit from being formed. The answer is that the operator in Tucson closes his end of the circuit by means of a switch called a *line switch*. When the operator in Tucson wants to answer the one in Cin-

cinnati, the Tucson operator opens his line switch and the Cincinnati operator closes his.

In a telephone, electric current causes an electromagnet to attract a metal disc that makes a sound. Let us see how this happens.

**How does a telephone work?**

Sound is made when some object moves back and forth very rapidly in air. This back-and-forth movement is called *vibration*. When an object vibrates, it pushes air outward from itself in a series of waves. When these air waves strike our ears, we hear a sound. For example, when you hit a drum, it vibrates and causes sound waves to move through the air to your ears. The sound that comes from a telephone receiver is also caused by vibration.

The telephone has two main parts. One is the mouthpiece, or *transmitter*, and the other is the *receiver*. You speak into the mouthpiece and hold the receiver to your ear.

Like all apparatus that uses electric current, the telephone must have a complete electrical circuit. When you dial a number, an automatic switch in the telephone exchange makes a circuit between your telephone and the telephone of the person you are calling. The telephone exchange also supplies the electricity for the circuit.

Inside the transmitter, there is a little round, flat box filled with grains of carbon. The top of this box is a thin metal disc. As you talk into the transmitter, the sound of your voice causes the metal disc to vibrate. The back-and-forth

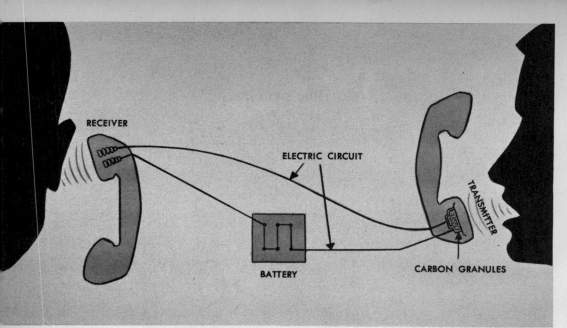

RECEIVER

ELECTRIC CIRCUIT

TRANSMITTER

BATTERY

CARBON GRANULES

Left, a simple telephone circuit with a battery. Below, a cutaway view of the telephone receiver showing the position of armature, permanent magnet, and electromagnet.

*(After diagrams, courtesy Bell Telephone Laboratories.)*

movement of the disc alternately presses the carbon grains together and then leaves them room to spread apart.

The grains of carbon are part of the electric circuit. Electricity can pass through the carbon grains more easily when they are pressed together than when they are spread apart. For this reason, the amount of electricity that passes the carbon grains changes from moment to moment as the disc vibrates.

This changing electric current passes along the wire to the receiver. In the receiver are an electromagnet and a metal disc. As the changing amount of electricity passes along the wire to the receiver, the electromagnet's pull varies from strong to weak. When the pull is strong, the disc is moved toward the electromagnet, and when the pull is weak, the disc springs away from the electromagnet. This back-and-forth movement of the disc causes air in front of the receiver to move back and forth in the same way. The vibrations of the disc cause sound waves to reach the ear that is held to the receiver. The sounds made by the receiver are the same as

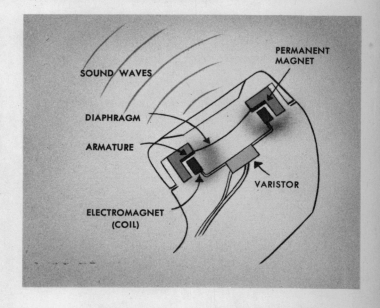

SOUND WAVES

PERMANENT MAGNET

DIAPHRAGM

ARMATURE

VARISTOR

ELECTROMAGNET (COIL)

those made by the voice at the other end of the wire.

The important thing to remember about a telephone is that it is not sound that travels along the wires. It is a changing amount of electricity that is caused by sound at the transmitter and is changed to sound by the receiver.

Using wood and small nails, build a wooden frame like the one in the illustration.

**How can you make a telegraph set?**

Before putting the frame together, ham-

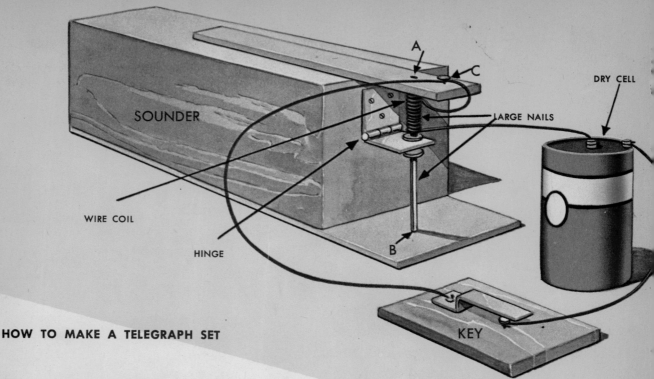

Labels on illustration: A, C, DRY CELL, SOUNDER, LARGE NAILS, WIRE COIL, HINGE, B, KEY

## HOW TO MAKE A TELEGRAPH SET

mer two large-headed nails into two of the pieces of wood at the points marked A and B in the illustration, and a small nail at C. The two nails must be in a straight line, and their heads must be only one-fourth of an inch apart. Wind a coil of wire in two or three layers around the upper nail and keep the wire in place with adhesive tape. Attach one end of the wire to one binding-post of a dry cell. Drive a small nail almost all the way into the top of the wooden frame. Attach to this nail the other end of the wire from the coil. Be sure to scrape the insulation off the ends of the wires before making connections.

Obtain a steel hinge  Make sure the hinge swings easily. If it doesn't, put a drop of oil into the cracks where the two halves of the hinge meet. Slip one half of the hinge between the heads of the two nails, as in the illustration. Nail or screw the other half of the hinge to the wooden frame, so that the unattached half of the hinge can move easily

up and down. (It may be easier to do this before you put the frame together.) This completes your sounder.

Connect two long wires to the switch you have been using in your experiments. The switch is now your telegraph key. Connect one of the wires to the nail on the top of the sounder. Connect the other wire to the second binding post of the dry cell. Your telegraph is complete.

Push the switch down and immediately let it up. The result is two clicks — one when the hinge flew up to hit the electromagnet (the upper nail) and the other when it fell back to the lower nail. By holding the switch down for a shorter or longer time, you can telegraph dots and dashes. By using the Morse code shown on page 45, you can telegraph messages.

## MORSE CODE

| | | |
|---|---|---|
| A · — | J · — — — | R · — · |
| B — · · · | K — · — | S · · · |
| C — · — · | L · — · · | T — |
| D — · · | M — — | U · · — |
| E · | N — · | V · · · — |
| F · · — · | O — — — | W · — — |
| G — — · | P · — — · | X — · · — |
| H · · · · | Q — — · — | Y — · — — |
| I · · | Z — — · · |

**How can you make a simple telephone?**

You will need the carbon rod from the center of a dead dry cell, the carbon rod from the center of a flashlight battery, a cigar box, a live dry cell, wires and an old telephone receiver or a set of earphones. Saw off two one-inch lengths of the carbon rod from the dead dry cell, and grind out a small hollow in the end of each piece. With sandpaper, sharpen the ends of the rod from the flashlight battery. Affix the two hollowed-out pieces of carbon to the back of the cigar box, using wire in the manner shown. The sharpened carbon rod should be placed between the two pieces of carbon, so that its points touch the hollowed-out place in each piece. Fasten a long piece of bell wire to each of the hollowed-out pieces of carbon, and run one wire to one pole of the live dry cell. Run the other wire to another room, where you connect it to the telephone

**HOW TO MAKE A SIMPLE TELEPHONE**

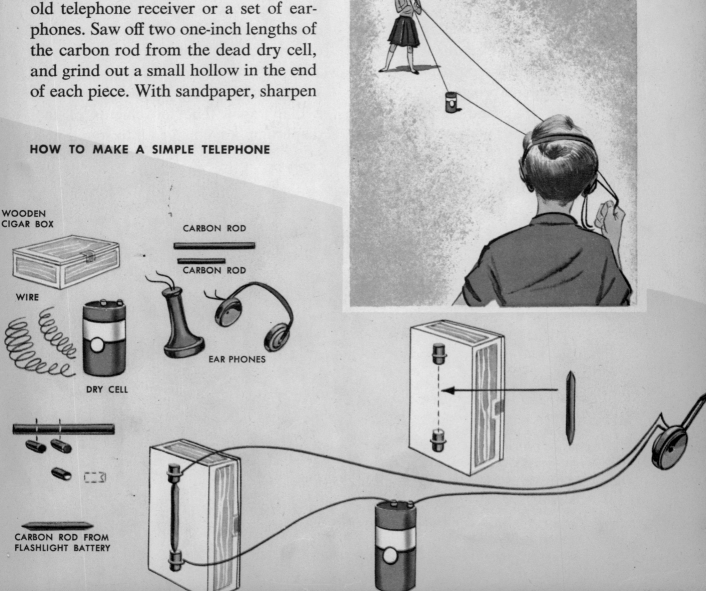

WOODEN CIGAR BOX

CARBON ROD

CARBON ROD

WIRE

DRY CELL

EAR PHONES

CARBON ROD FROM FLASHLIGHT BATTERY

receiver or headphones. Take a third wire and connect the other pole of the dry cell with the receiver, as the illustration shows. Your telephone is complete. If someone talks into the front of the cigar box, the movement of the sharpened carbon rod will vary the amount of electric current in the wires, and the diaphragm of the receiver will vibrate to produce the same sound waves as those of the person speaking into the box.

We learned that an electric current in a wire produces a magnetic field. If the amount of current is varied, the strength of the field varies. If you have the proper electronic apparatus, you can broadcast the variations of the magnetic field. This is exactly what is done in radio and

**What part do magnets play in radio and television?**

television broadcasting. The broadcast variations are called *electromagnetic waves*. The electronic equipment in radio and television sets can detect the electromagnetic waves at long distances from where they are broadcast. Let us see how this works.

A microphone in a broadcasting studio is much like a transmitter in a telephone. Sound waves enter the microphone and cause it to vary the strength of electrical impulses. These impulses produce magnetic fields of varying strength, and the variations are broadcast as electromagnetic waves that we call radio waves. When these electromagnetic waves reach a radio, electronic equipment changes them into electric current of varying strength. This varying electric current varies the strength of an electromagnet that moves a diaphragm. The movements of the diaphragm are changed into sound just

Did you ever realize how important a part magnets and magnetism play in radio and TV broadcasting and receiving, tape recording, and the making of phonograph records?

as in a telephone receiver. So, you can see that the "sound" that is broadcast to a radio receiver is really a series of electromagnetic waves that are changed into sound by the action of an electromagnet. A television set has a radio inside its cabinet to reproduce sounds broadcast from the television studio.

A television picture also depends on magnets. When a television camera focuses on an object, light reflected from the object enters the lens of the camera and falls on a screen, which is inside a large glass tube. Also inside the tube is an electron gun that shoots a moving beam of electrons at the screen. The beam sweeps back and forth across the screen from top to bottom, 30 times a second. This is called *scanning*. The path of the moving beam is controlled by electromagnets. The beam is affected differently by the light and dark areas on the screen across which it sweeps.

These differences are changed into varying electromagnetic waves that are then broadcast.

The television receiver in your home has a large electronic tube something like the one in the television camera. It, too, has a magnetically-controlled electron gun and scans a screen in the tube. Actually, two electron beams scan the screen, each making 525 separate horizontal lines 30 times a second. You surely have seen these light and dark lines on the screen of your television set. The screen is at the front of the tube and is made of a chemical substance that glows more or less brightly, depending on the strength of the electron beam that strikes it. The variations in brightness match the variations in light that enter the television camera. As a result, the picture on your television screen matches the objects on which the television camera is focused.

# You and Magnetism

You have learned much about magnetism, but you, and the best scientists in the world, cannot explain magnetism very well. No one knows how to connect his observations of magnetism with other scientific knowledge, and thereby clarify the nature of magnetism. Seeking these connections between magnetism and other knowledge, seeking to explain why magnetism exerts a force and why it seems to exist in all known parts of the universe, and discovering many other things about magnetism offer you a lifetime of fascinating work. Applying magnetism in scientific research and in inventions offers another interesting field of work. For example, you probably know that there are a few places in the world where electricity is being generated from atomic energy. These atomic energy machines, called *atomic reactors,* require expensive fuel that is obtained from the rare chemical element, uranium. There is a better and cheaper way to obtain atomic energy: by harnessing the vast power of the hydrogen bomb. To do this, scientists must use a very thin, but extremely hot gas at temperatures measured in hundreds of millions of degrees. This gas is called a *plasma.* No material can hold anything as hot as plasma. However, atomic scientists are trying to hold it in a magnetic bottle, which is a bottle-shaped magnetic field. They have found this to be very difficult. So far, magnetic bottles have been able to hold the plasma for only a few thousandths of a second. Perhaps you will be the one to invent a magnetic bottle that can hold plasma as long as you wish. If you do, you will perform a great service to mankind. You will make possible cheap and safe atomic energy that will generate electricity for people in parts of the world where it cannot now be made.

So far, magnetic bottles have been able to hold the plasma for only a few thousandths of a second.

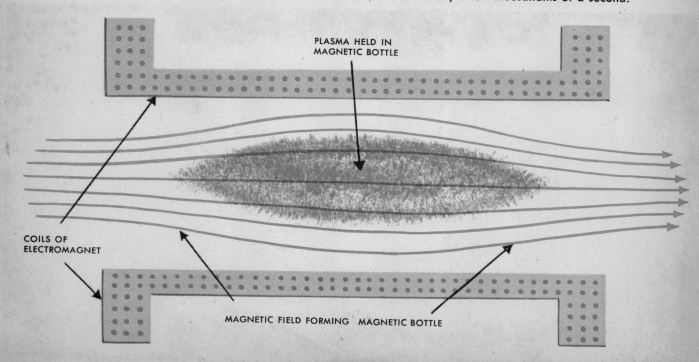

PLASMA HELD IN
MAGNETIC BOTTLE

COILS OF
ELECTROMAGNET

MAGNETIC FIELD FORMING  MAGNETIC BOTTLE